GHP

Emma's **E** Book

WRITTEN BY **J. L. MAZZEO**
ILLUSTRATED BY **HELEN ROSS REVUTSKY**

dingles & company New Jersey

First Printing

Published By dingles&company
P.O. Box 508
Sea Girt, New Jersey 08750

LIBRARY OF CONGRESS CATALOG CARD NUMBER
2005907190

ISBN
ISBN-13: 978 1-59646-440-7
ISBN-10: 1-59646-440-2

Printed in the United States of America

My Letter Library series is based on the original concept of Judy Mazzeo Zocchi.

ART DIRECTION
Barbie Lambert & Rizco Design
DESIGN
Rizco Design
EDITED BY
Andrea Curley
PROJECT MANAGER
Lisa Aldorasi
EDUCATIONAL CONSULTANT
Maura Ruane McKenna
PRE-PRESS BY
Pixel Graphics

EXPLORE THE LETTERS OF THE ALPHABET WITH MY LETTER LIBRARY*

Aimee's **A** Book
Bebe's **B** Book
Cassie's **C** Book
Delia's **D** Book
Emma's **E** Book
Faye's **F** Book
George's **G** Book
Henry's **H** Book
Izzy's **I** Book
Jade's **J** Book
Kelsey's **K** Book
Logan's **L** Book
Mia's **M** Book
Nate's **N** Book
Owen's **O** Book
Peter's **P** Book
Quinn's **Q** Book
Rosie's **R** Book
Sofie's **S** Book
Tad's **T** Book
Uri's **U** Book
Vera's **V** Book
Will's **W** Book
Xavia's **X** Book
Yola's **Y** Book
Zach's **Z** Book

* All titles also available in bilingual English/Spanish versions.

WEBSITE
www.dingles.com
E-MAIL
info@dingles.com

My Letter Library leads young children through the alphabet one letter at a time. By focusing on an individual letter in each book, the series allows youngsters to identify and absorb the concept of each letter thoroughly before being introduced to the next. In addition, it invites them to look around and discover where objects beginning with the specific letter appear in their own world.

Ee

A a   B b   C c   D d   **E e**   F f   G g

H h   I i   J j   K k   L l   M m   N n

O o   P p   Q q   R r   S s   T t   U u

V v   W w   X x   Y y   Z z

E is for Emma.

Emma is

an elegant elephant.

Near Emma's blanket
you might see an **e**nvelope,

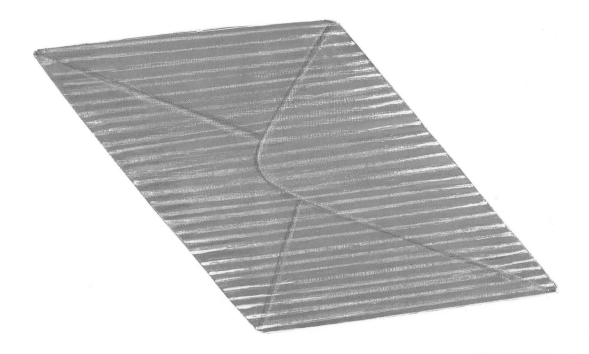

Ee

a pink eraser,

E e

or an **e**ight on a box.

E e

Close to Emma
you might find **e**lderberries,

Ee

a purple **e**ggplant

from Emma's garden,

Ee

and an **e**gg in an **e**gg cup
to eat for breakfast.

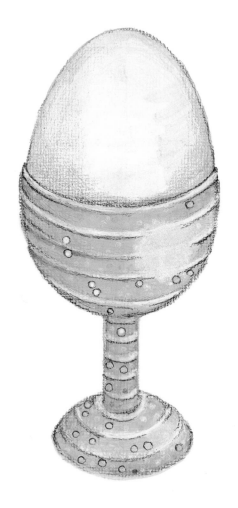

Ee

On the ground by Emma
you might spot an **e**arwig,

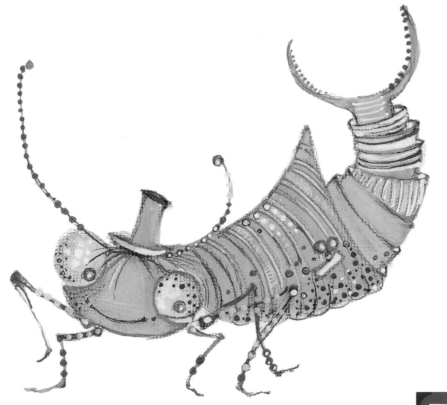

E e

an **e**arthworm

crawling home,

E e

or an easy-going **e**lf.

Ee

Things that begin with
the letter **E** are all around.

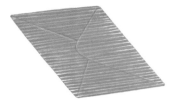

ENVELOPE

ERASER

EIGHT

ELDERBERRIES

EGGPLANT

EGG, **E**GG CUP

EARWIG

EARTHWORM

ELF

Where in Emma's backyard
can they be found?

Have an "E" Day!

Read "E" stories all day long.
Read books about erasers, eggplants, eggs, earthworms, and other **E** words. Then have the child pick out all of the words and pictures starting with the letter **E**.

Make an "E" Craft: An Eggshell E
Trace a large letter **E** on construction paper. Let the child cut out the **E** with a pair of scissors.

The next time you have eggs for breakfast or make hard-boiled eggs, save some of the eggshells.

Wash the eggshells thoroughly and let them dry completely.

Have the child crush the eggshells into small pieces.

Have him or her spread glue on the cutout **E** and then press the eggshells onto the glue.

After the glue dries, hang up your eggceptional **"E"**!

Make an "E" Snack: Eggplant Slices
- Wash and dry an eggplant thoroughly.
- Cut it into thin slices widthwise.
- Have the child arrange the slices on a cookie sheet.
- Sprinkle olive oil over the tops of the slices.
- Bake in a preheated oven at 375 degrees F for 20 minutes.
- After the slices have baked, let them cool. Then let the child sprinkle them with Parmesan cheese or salt—and enjoy!

For additional **"E"** Day ideas and a reading list, go to www.dingles.com.

About **Letters**

Use the My Letter Library series to teach a child to identify letters and recognize the sounds they make by hearing them used and repeated in each story.

Ask:
- What letter is this book about?
- Can you name all of the **E** pictures on each page?
- Which **E** picture is your favorite? Why?
- Can you find all of the words in this book that begin with the letter **E**?

ENVIRONMENT
Discuss objects that begin with the letter **E** in the child's immediate surroundings and environment.

Use these questions to further the conversation:
- Do you like to eat eggs? If so, how do you like them prepared?
- Have you ever tried eggplant?
- If so, did you like it? How did it taste?
- Have you ever seen an elephant in person?
- If so, where?

OBSERVATIONS
The My Letter Library series can be used to enhance the child's imagination. Encourage the child to look around and tell you what he or she sees.

Ask:
- Where do elephants live?
- Pretend that you are an elephant—walk around your room, using your arm as if it were an elephant's trunk.
- Can you find eight **E** objects inside or outside of your house?
- What is your favorite **E** object at home? Why?

TRY SOMETHING NEW...
Ask your parent if you can help plant a garden or do yard work. Count how many earthworms you come across while you are working, but be careful not to hurt them!

J. L. MAZZEO grew up in Middletown, New Jersey, as part of a close-knit Italian American family. She currently resides in Monmouth County, New Jersey, and still remains close to family members in heart and home.

HELEN ROSS REVUTSKY was born in St. Petersburg, Russia, where she received a degree in stage artistry/design. She worked as the directing artist in Kiev's famous Governmental Puppet Theatre. Her first book, *I Can Read the Alphabet,* was published in Moscow in 1998. Helen now lives in London, where she has illustrated several children's books.